Arctic Animals
Life Outside the Igloo

Polar Bear

by Dee Phillips

Consultants:

Alysa McCall, Field Programs Manager
Polar Bears International, Winnipeg, Manitoba, Canada

Barbara Nielsen, Director of Communications
Polar Bears International, Winnipeg, Manitoba, Canada

Kimberly Brenneman, PhD
National Institute for Early Education Research, Rutgers University, New Brunswick, New Jersey

BEARPORT
PUBLISHING

New York, New York

Credits

Cover, © FloridaStock/Shutterstock; 2–3, © Eric Isselee/Shutterstock; 4, © Matthias Breiter/Minden Pictures/FLPA; 5, © Mitsuaki Iwago/Minden Pictures/FLPA; 7, © Konrad Wothe/Minden Pictures/FLPA; 8, © mycteria/Shutterstock; 9, © Flip Nicklin/Minden Pictures/FLPA; 10, © National Geographic Images Collection/Alamy; 11, © Arco Images Gmbh/Alamy; 12, © Don Land/Shutterstock; 13, © Mitsuaki Iwago/Minden Pictures/FLPA; 14T, © Jenny E. Ross/Corbis; 14B, © J.L. Klein and M.L. Hubert/FLPA; 15, © outdoorsman/Shutterstock; 16, © André Gilden/Alamy; 17, © Belovodchenko Anton/Shutterstock; 18T, © Sergey Gorshkov/Minden Pictures/FLPA; 18B, © Alaska Stock/Alamy; 19, © Matthias Breiter/Minden Pictures/FLPA; 20, © Shchipkova Elena/Shutterstock; 21, © Konrad Wothe/Minden Pictures/FLPA; 23TC, © Maxim Petrichuk/Shutterstock; 23TR, © AEPhotographic/Shutterstock; 23BL, © Matthias Breiter/Minden Pictures/FLPA; 23BC, © Milkovasa/Shutterstock; 23BR, © gevision/Shutterstock.

Publisher: Kenn Goin
Creative Director: Spencer Brinker
Editor: Jessica Rudolph
Photo Researcher: Ruby Tuesday Ltd

Library of Congress Cataloging-in-Publication Data

Phillips, Dee, 1967– author.
 Polar bear / by Dee Phillips.
     pages cm. — (Arctic animals : life outside the igloo)
 Includes bibliographical references and index.
 ISBN 978-1-62724-526-5 (library binding : alk. paper) — ISBN 1-62724-526-X (library binding : alk. paper)
 1. Polar bear—Juvenile literature. 2. Arctic regions—Juvenile literature. I. Title.
 QL737.C27P47 2015
 599.786—dc23

                              2014036508

For more information, write to Bearport Publishing Company, Inc., 45 West 21st Street, Suite 3B, New York, New York 10010. Printed in the United States of America.

10 9 8 7 6 5 4 3 2 1

Contents

Welcome to the Arctic

It's a spring morning in one of the coldest places on Earth—the **Arctic**.

A huge female polar bear crawls out of her **den**.

Her two tiny babies follow her outside.

For months, the den has protected the bears from the freezing winter weather.

Now the bear cubs follow their mother as she looks for food.

polar bear cub

den

4

female polar bear

An adult female polar bear weighs up to 650 pounds (295 kg). A male bear may weigh 1,200 pounds (544 kg)—as much as eight adult humans!

cub

A Polar Bear's World

In the polar bear's Arctic home, the land is covered in ice and snow.

The ocean is so cold that part of its surface is frozen all year.

This large island of floating ice is called the Arctic ice cap.

In winter, the ice cap grows bigger as more of the ocean freezes.

Sometimes the ice joins up with the **shore**.

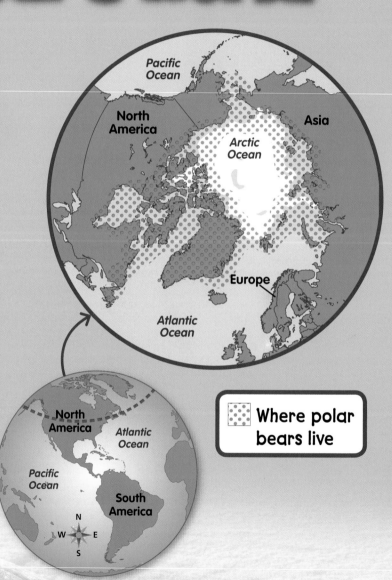

Pacific Ocean

North America

Asia

Arctic Ocean

Europe

Atlantic Ocean

North America

Atlantic Ocean

Pacific Ocean

South America

N W E S

:::: Where polar bears live

How Does a Bear Stay Warm?

A polar bear has two layers of fur that keep it warm.

The top layer of fur is long and thick.

The next layer, called the undercoat, is short and woolly.

Under the bear's fur is a thick layer of fat.

The fat also helps keep the polar bear warm.

thick fur

The bottoms of a polar bear's paws are covered with fur and bumpy pads. The pads and fur grip the ice and snow. This prevents the bear from slipping when it walks.

bumpy pads

A polar bear's paw measures about 12 inches (30.5 cm) in width. What item can you find that is about the same size as a polar bear's paw?

9

Hungry Bears

Polar bears spend lots of time searching for food.

Their main food is ringed seals.

An adult polar bear mostly just eats the part of a seal's fat called **blubber**.

The fatty blubber gives the bear lots of energy and helps keep it warm.

Polar bears also eat walruses, seabirds, and dead whales that get washed up onto the shore.

whale bones

An adult polar bear can eat 100 pounds (45 kg) of seal blubber in one meal. It often leaves the meat and bones. Arctic foxes and young polar bears feed on these leftovers.

arctic fox

seal bones

Seals live mostly in the ocean. How do you think polar bears catch them?

Hunting for Seals

Polar bears hunt for seals on the frozen ocean.

First, a bear finds a hole in the ice.

Then it waits—sometimes for hours.

Finally, a seal pops up from the hole to take a breath of air.

The bear hits and kills the seal with its giant, powerful paws.

Then it drags the dead animal from the water using its paws and teeth.

a hole in the ice

Sometimes, seals rest on the ice. If a polar bear spots a seal, it slowly crawls toward the animal on its belly. The bear's white fur helps it blend in with the ice. The seal doesn't see the bear. Once the bear is close, it attacks!

dead seal

A Bear's Everyday Life

Polar bears may walk for hundreds of miles in a year looking for seals.

They also swim from one huge chunk of floating ice to another.

Their huge paws act like paddles in the water.

An adult bear can swim all day before getting tired.

When it wants to rest, it climbs onto the ice and lies down.

a polar bear swimming in the sea

a polar bear resting on the ice

There are often heavy snowstorms called **blizzards** in the Arctic. During a blizzard, a bear digs a shallow hole in the thick ice or snow and climbs in. Soon, the bear is covered with falling snow. The bear stays buried until the storm passes.

a bear sleeping in a snowstorm

A Den for Baby Bears

Adult polar bears spend most of their time alone.

In late spring, however, male and female bears meet up to **mate**.

In late fall, a female bear digs a den under the snow.

Then, she climbs inside and spends most of the winter sleeping.

In November or December, she gives birth to one, two, or three cubs inside the den.

a female polar bear digging a den

A newborn polar bear cub is about 14 inches (36 cm) long, from its nose to its rear end. It weighs just one pound (0.5 kg).

Little Polar Bears

Inside the den, the cubs stay warm by cuddling up to their huge mom.

They drink milk from her body.

The cubs grow bigger and stronger.

When spring arrives, the bear family leaves the den.

The baby bears see their icy world for the first time.

They explore and play in the snow.

polar bear cubs playing in the snow

A mother polar bear eats nothing all winter. She's able to stay alive because her body uses up its fat.

mother bear

a cub drinking milk

19

Bear Lessons

After leaving the den, the hungry mother bear soon heads for the floating ice.

The cubs learn how to catch seals by watching her hunt.

The babies still drink milk, though, until they are about 20 months old.

When the cubs are two to three years old, they leave their mother.

Now they are ready to be grown-up polar bears.

Polar bear cubs learn how to swim by following their mother. When she jumps into the water, the babies join her. The little bears splash around until they figure out how to swim.

The people who live in the Arctic have given polar bears many names. They are known as sea bears, ice bears, and white bears. Think of a new name for the bears that tells something about these animals.

mother bear

six-month-old cubs

Science Lab

Keeping Warm

Check out how fat keeps a polar bear warm with this investigation.

> **You will need:**
> • A small bowl • Water • Lots of ice cubes
> • A towel • Empty balloons

1. Fill a bowl with cold water and ice cubes.

2. Put your right pointer finger into the icy water. Hold it there for 30 seconds. Remove your finger from the water and dry it.

   How did your finger feel when it was in the water?

3. Now put a balloon over your left pointer finger.

Do you think this finger will feel colder, warmer, or the same when it's in the water?

4. Now place both pointer fingers in the icy water. Keep them there for 30 seconds.

   How does each finger feel?

   What is happening to the finger that's covered with the balloon?

   How could you make your left pointer finger feel even less cold in the water?

(The answers are on page 24.)

22

Science Words

Arctic (ARK-tik) the northernmost area on Earth, which includes the Arctic Ocean and the North Pole

blizzards (BLIZ-urdz) storms with strong winds and blowing snow

blubber (BLUH-bur) a layer of fat under the skin of animals such as seals and whales

den (DEN) a home where wild animals can rest, be safe, and have babies

mate (MAYT) to come together in order to have young

shore (SHOR) the land along the edge of a river, lake, or ocean

Index

Read More

Kolpin, Molly. *Polar Bears (First Facts).* North Mankato, MN: Capstone Press (2012).

Owen, Ruth. *Polar Bear Cubs (Wild Baby Animals).* New York: Bearport (2011).

Shea, Therese. *Bears.* New York: PowerKids Press (2007).

Learn More Online

To learn more about polar bears, visit **www.bearportpublishing.com/ArcticAnimals**

About the Author

Dee Phillips lives near the ocean on the southwest coast of England. She develops and writes nonfiction and fiction books for children of all ages.

Answers for Page 22

The finger covered with a balloon is insulated, or protected, from the icy water by the balloon. It feels less cold than the uncovered finger. The balloon acted like a polar bear's fat. The bear's fat insulates its body against icy water and cold weather. If you put two or three balloons onto your left pointer finger, it will feel even less cold!